Wrestling with Toxicity

OrangeBooks Publication

Website: www.orangebooks.in

First Edition 2025

Cover Design by Veeksha Vagmita

ISBN: 978-93-6554-346-9

Price: Rs. 300.00

Printed in India

Wrestling with Toxicity

Word-Wounds, Warped Webs

Dialogues, Monologues & Satire in Verse

VEEKSHA VAGMITA

OrangeBooks Publication
www.orangebooks.in

Dedicated with Deep Gratitude to The Ones Who Saw in Me the Strength I Didn't Know I Possessed

Contents

Disclaimer: This collection explores intense issues like abuse and toxic dynamics. It is recommended for readers who are 18 years old or above.

A Note to the Readers

The first draft of the poems in this collection was written to survive the emotional abuse I have faced both online and offline. In the process of transferring my psychological load onto paper, I wrote something brimming with raw emotions, which were buried deep within. I was not certain if everyone would be able to relate to my experiences, but I had a feeling that this collection of poems needed to be published for broadening people's understanding of abuse and toxic dynamics. The poems evolved as I applied myself to this work, revealing the parallels between the microcosm and the macrocosm: the difference lay only in the magnitude of abuse and the range of its manifestations. Consequently, the poetry was transmuted into something that simultaneously encapsulated and transcended the personal.

This gave the verses inspired by particular experiences more weight, greater relatability and a larger scope.

That is when I decided to turn my poetic creations, written as a coping mechanism, into a book that could possibly help others grappling with the toxicity emanating from abuse or difficult dynamics. I fervently hope that those who find themselves in such a predicament draw strength from the commonalities between their struggles and mine. Things change when we realize that our trials and tribulations are not a peculiar curse but the result of a widespread menace. It is something we may have been dimly aware of all along, but when that reality sinks in, it is truly empowering. These poems have been written to help that reality sink in. The poison spreading through social media can have a far-reaching impact.

This collection takes a gritty look at the grim reality of our times. The avalanche of toxicity on social media mirrors and magnifies the hatred infecting hearts and minds in the real world. This is an issue that calls for serious and sustained engagement. Hopefully, we shall overcome the digital onslaught that, despite its undeniable benefits, has been terribly disruptive.

These poems, written in the depths of despair, took me by surprise. They flowed out of me in a state of sublime, seething madness. In a way, the poem wrote themselves. Having written poems enough to form a collection, I felt an inner prompting to share them with the world. I was deeply convinced of the need to help people expand their understanding of the nature and pervasiveness of abuse: the scourge and besetting sin of our age.

Abuse can often of go undetected owing to a lack of awareness of its pathological manifestations, to the detriment of unsuspecting victims woefully unprepared to handle what's coming their way. I seek to unpack this pernicious phenomenon in the hope that you may be able to identify abuse in its varying guises: covert or overt. Don't be overwhelmed if you have the grave misfortune of encountering abuse in any form. Empower yourself to detect it quickly, no matter how subtle it is.

Don't wonder why it happened to *you*. It happens to many people and it is not—I repeat, it is NOT—about YOU. The problem is not with you but with those who perpetrate and perpetuate abuse. Remind yourself of your indisputable worth and incalculable value as a human being. Tell your story to empathic listeners. If you feel the need for it, take help from a competent therapist to regain your confidence. Read up on this widespread but inadequately understood menace. Abuse is nothing but an expression of irrational hatred. Don't try to make sense of it. Just save yourself from it and equip others to shield themselves too.

In addition to diving deep into the murky waters of abusive dynamics, I offer portraits of relationships that, despite appearing smooth, have hidden rough edges that end up bruising us all too often. Still, we try to put up with the abrasiveness built into the texture of connections that go far back in time. We take the discomfort in our stride and accept it as a familiar irritant. But there are times when we can't deny the need to put those relationships under the microscope and identify the toxic patterns we've been ignoring from the force of habit—patterns that have dented our psyche with their stubborn repetitiveness. That's when we confront the reality, depressing though it may be, that, much as we would want to, we cannot mend or salvage every relationship. Like love, every relationship takes two. And sometimes, it's just you, straining every sinew to get through to the other person, who is blithely indifferent to the litany of woes you need to give voice to. If only they would listen. Quite often, they don't. That can either sound the death knell of the relationship or change things beyond repair. There's no going back to the way things were.

Not every personal equation can be reset to make it comfortable for both the parties involved. Sooner or later, we come to terms with this hard reality. Our psyche revolts. The toxicity that was accepted as a given can no longer be endured. What we first dimly suspected, then quietly tolerated, then mildly resisted, is ultimately, outrightly rejected.

The poems in this collection tackle a difficult issue. I take a gritty look at toxic human dynamics through poetic dialogues, monologues and commentary. The poems present the point of view of victims, abusers, enablers and observers. One poem, titled "Well-intentioned Souls?", is written from the point of view of a critical observer of the drama of abuse. The topic of this poetry collection demanded a trenchant exploration of a troubling issue. The tone and tenor of the poetry reflects that trenchancy. I hope this collection provokes reflections on a very difficult dimension of human dynamics.

We often think of poetry as a song, a flower, a thing of beauty—rendered charmingly in words. But poetry must also evoke the thorns, the trauma, the toxicity, that leave our lives in disarray. It is profoundly challenging to depict what is inherently unpoetic through the medium of verse. I can only hope that I have accomplished this with some degree of success and that the reader will find something worthwhile in this excruciating labour of love.

Veeksha Vagmita

That element of tragedy which lies in the very fact of frequency, has not yet wrought itself into the coarse emotion of mankind; and perhaps our frames could hardly bear much of it. If we had a keen vision and feeling of all ordinary human life, it would be like hearing the grass grow and the squirrel's heart beat, and we should die of that roar which lies on the other side of silence.

George Eliot, *Middlemarch*

Prologue

A Victim Finding Her Voice

Who am I?

I don't really know

A cat or a human, I'm not so sure

My self-image has become a mishmash

of attributes dumped into my supposed core

The Real Me is smudged and tarred

besides being deeply scarred.

Sometimes I wonder how any person could be

An angel one day, the devil the next

Unless they suspect me of shape-shifting

Or are just speaking in jest

But that they are not

Even if it makes your jaw drop.

If nothing else fits,

I become the "clown in town"

Maybe they can't tell jokes from jibes

Or are brimming with spite.

If I howl in anguish, I am unstable

If I suffer in silence, my pain becomes invisible

If I am patient, the suffering never ends

If I protest, the locusts descend.

I don't know what my tormentors expect?

Should I smile in approval

when they decide I'm delusional

because that dovetails nicely

with the story they want to tell?

If it gives them peace,

I'll gladly proclaim—

Hey people, I'm insane!

I'm sorry if I don't look the part

Or if your perception is too coloured

to see what's right before your eyes.

Underneath the layers of grime

deposited on me over a harrowing stretch of time

lies a person doing reasonably fine—

a miracle that boggles even *my* mind.

I've pulled myself together with humungous effort

after being derailed umpteen times.

If *I* can see *you*, flaws and all

Why can't you see me too?

There's no mystery here to be solved

Or any conundrum to be resolved

You've tied yourself up in knots

By forgetting a simple fact—

I'm distinct, just like you

Just like you, I'm a person with imperfections

Imperfections that are a part of being human

And, in my own way, I am special

Just like you are.

The air is charged with rumours

Though I want to block my ears,

your poisonous words worm their way

into my already befuddled brain.

And I have an excruciating headache.

Once again.

If I could ward off these irritants,

it would spare me the torment

of listening to the rubbish

being bandied about merrily.

You call me a wild, witchy mad cat

who will pounce on you at the drop of a hat.

I don't know what's the matter with you

I have much better things to do.

I'm curious to see the crazy cat masquerading as me

But I think I'll just let it be.

I heard someone complaining about

my non-existent paws

that I might put on a person they jealously guard.

From what angle do I look like a cat?

Since when did I grow whiskers?

The last time I checked the mirror,

it begged to differ.

There's no resemblance whatsoever

between me and that four-legged creature

known for chasing mice.

Just for your information,

I like to keep a safe distance

from rats, lizards, cockroaches, ants, spiders ...

You can add more to the list,

if you so wish.

Such a barrage of nonsense is an assault on one's imagination

How happy I'd be to simply dismiss it as a hallucination

That way, I'll be spared the agony

of encountering all things cranky.

And you call into question my sanity?

Seriously?

Everything seems topsy-turvy

Reason has been turned on its head

And yet, whatever goes wrong is given a reason

And that reason, for some reason, is always me

even if that requires you to twist reality.

Please don't attack me

if I point out something you fail to see.

While you were puzzling over ... God knows what

Reason got fed up and left the building.

Wait! Don't press the panic button so quickly

Rumour will continue to do your bidding

Who cares about this bloody Reason?

Rumour is the flavour of the season.

If you're angry with Reason's audacity,

you can always take your frustration out on me.

Don't worry, I won't make the mistake of asking

"Why?"

Your answer will surely turn my head into a jelly

And I'm ferociously protective of my sanity.

Sorry to disappoint you but I'm NOT crazy.

Part 1

Simply Toxic

1

As if Words Were Bullets!

An Abuser Dismisses Word-Wounds

Words, mere words, gentler than a beating
Soft like an infant's palm, smooth like satin
Charged like a loaded gun, ready for firing
Needing no trigger, just some clever play
That twists them enough to warp their meaning
And unleash their venom on the victim.

It's not very hard
If you've perfected this diabolical art
Just open your sharp-shooting mouth
And watch your words accomplish the task.

If your timing is perfect

You'll hit your target

At the right spot

With deadly effect

Deadlier than shooting

A bullet through their head.

Oh, these bloodless word-crimes

must never be condemned!

They're the next best thing to non-violence

Without dirtying your hands

They meet your ghastly ends

Sparing you the horror

Of seeing the wounds you've left

No burden of guilt, no need for shame

Because, you see, there's nothing to blame!

Not a single scar to prove the offence

Because no offence was ever meant

Or let me just say it straight

I know how to offend without leaving a trace

So, you can whine all you want

But it would make no difference.

So, what if I let out a stream of poisonous words?

In fact, they are rather innocuous

It's not my fault if you have such flimsy nerves

If you have to survive, you've got to be tough

Getting shattered by injuries inflicted by *words*?

Are you serious?

If words leave you bruised

You're nothing but a buffoon

Why should words always mean well?

They can mean other things too.

And if you find them hollow from within

Why don't you stuff them with your own meaning?

If even words were scrutinised like weapons

Silence will descend on the whole universe

So, let there be a carnival of words

Let them crawl under your skin like worms

That's how freedom of speech is ultimately won

It's a liberation most ardently to be desired

Why stop people from venting their murderous ire?

Do you want *real* bullets to be fired?

Block your ears if you're feeling sick and torn

But let the riotous word-slay go on.

PS: Wounds that are visible are recognised far more easily than those deep within. However, psychological injuries are no less serious and merit equal attention. Cruel words can hit the psyche like a bullet. These word-wounds tend to be easily dismissed, especially by abusers, because they are hidden from view. Here's a poem, written with scathing wit, that illustrates an abuser's easy dismissal of the terrible wounds they've inflicted with words chosen deliberately to cause pain. The poem highlights emotional violence—both online and offline—perpetrated by words.

I'm grateful to the ThePrint for publishing this poem.

2

No Method, Only Madness

A Victim Confronts Her Tormentor

Do you have hobbies other than spinning yarns

and doling out theory after theory

to force-fit reality into the stories

you contrive with dizzying rapidity

to score your silly points?

Every day, there's a new claim

Desperately seeking to maim

a person already limping through life.

Dragging out your bizarre game

Is there something called shame?

Recruiting people to spout your nonsense

Coercing them to keep their distance

as if I was some kind of virus

that will infect people

by living a normal life.

Looks like the sky will go up in flames

if I have my space and socialise.

So, every day you find a reason

to justify my isolation.

Keeping me in an invisible prison

for no conceivable reason.

Even when I plumb the depths of despair,

you continue to wage your imaginary war

against what is just and eminently fair.

Have you not run out of ideas

to malign my image, my very being?

How much muck will you fling

in the hope that something sticks?

Every day, you try new tricks

designed to make me trip.

Hoping that one day

I will be too tired

to pick myself up

and have my say.

No longer will I have the strength

to live my life *my* way.

You want to have the final word

Don't worry, my friend

Have some patience

The fight has almost gone out of me

I would suggest you begin your preparations

to celebrate your "victory",

whatever that means in your lexicon.

I'm almost on the brink

The day is not far

when I and my dreams will be gone with the wind.

So, take it easy

And enjoy your drink.

3

Why Abuse?

A Victim and an Abuser Have a War of Words

Abuse?

Just abuse!

Just like that?

You want excuse?

You want reason?

Apology?

Justification!

You must be kidding

You really don't know how it works?

Abuse is its own justification

Like virtue is its own reward.

Don't frown, you idiot

I mean every word

And you better take me seriously

Because I'm knowledgeable to a fault.

This is simply absurd

If you won't throw a fit,

I'll show you how it works.

But I don't think I'll be heard

So, I won't waste my words.

Listen, I'm not a dolt

I can tell that you love nothing more

than to hear yourself speak.

Doling out pearls of wisdom

that nobody in the world needs.

If you stand on the stage and preach

I bet, no one will give a fig.

I beg to differ.

My words are measured

My arguments coherent

My tone is controlled

I have done nothing to be mocked and trolled.

You think I owe you a response

for the abuse that is well-deserved.

As a matter of fact, you do.

Stop mewling like a baby

Grow up, you drama queen

Look within

What are you doing

to force people to stoop to such lengths?

Oh God! What are you doing to draw out the worst

in people who won't even want to hurt an insect?

Why do you get so easily worked up?

Your very existence is the bane of this world!

Your blood-shot eyes, your clenched fist,

proclaim your self-triggered malice.

Go away! You self-pitying dimwit.

Why are you determined to tear me to bits?

How tiring it is to get rid

of even a speck of dirt!

In case you didn't get the clue,

it's a reference to YOU.

Yes, you got that right.

That speck of dirt is "You".

You and your ilk deserve to be kicked in the butt

And yet, I try my best to ignore you pests

But you give me no credit for my restraint

I give you enough time to breathe ...

Before I strike again.

So, what's your bloody problem then?

You've called me a clown, a b*tch, a mad cat.

Oh, so you take offence to offensive language!

Since when was "bitch" an insult?

I use it as an endearment for my female friends

Not for you though

With you, I'm in deadly earnest.

You think I didn't get it?

It's amazing how you seek to defend what you do

with such an obvious intent.

And since you're so eager to offend,

I'll pave the way for you to say

whatever pops into your head.

Swear, fret, fume, scream ...

I will, by all means

And if I feel like it,

I will scream till you take to your heels

So, you better keep your mouth shut

It's in your best interest

Don't tempt me to bare my fangs

You don't know who I am

I can offend to my heart's content

And not a leaf will stir in protest.

By the way, what's wrong in abusing

the bleeding hearts

feeling for every bloody cause?

We're ruining the world

with all these crusaders, truth-tellers,

Good Samaritans, whatever.

It's time we stop pampering

these silly do-gooders

bent on protecting the cry-babies

and the weaklings

unfit to handle the slings

of a fate

determined by the high and mighty,

whose word alone carries weight.

Have you spewed all the venom

coursing through your veins?

Looks like there's more coming my way ...

Yes, you moron, I'm not yet done

If abuse is the destiny of some

useless cat, dog, human ...

Why do you create such a mayhem?

If they're drowning in pain,

it must be the grand design

If their suffering,

which they must have brought upon themselves,

fools that they are,

is killing their very soul,

that must be God's will.

He's the one who takes the call

Not me.

Oh, please spare God at least

Don't drag Him into this bullsh*t

You'll do well to control your tongue a bit.

For your benefit,

I'll repeat my words—

It's not me. It's not me.

It's God who decides everything.

I don't run the world.

It's God. Not me.

Not me. Not me.

Heard it?

Clearly?

Remember it.

Or I'll remind you daily.

Even a toddler is not so prickly
And you call others "cry-babies"?
Why do you shift the blame for your devilry?
Are you afraid of taking responsibility?

Afraid? Me?
Not even in your wildest dreams!
I'm stronger than steel
with a great sense of responsibility.
I keep people in their place
so that no dares to dream
of a world infected with fairness.
To hell with democracy, diversity
and all that claptrap!
Let the mighty rule with strictness
and use every means

for their worthy ends.

All that I can gather from your tiresome tirade

is that there is no end to your meaningless hatred.

I know how to set straight

you and your kind,

the scourge of this age—

Insult, abuse, malign, isolate

Banish all talk

of making amends,

of healing the trauma of battered brains,

of rescuing the ones in the crosshairs

of those understandably intent on causing pain.

Won't it be insane

to feel sorry for a cockroach meant to be squashed?

It's the worthless creature's fate

What? Do not look at me with such disdain

Those who know the art of abuse

are also spurred on by their muse.

Never heard anything more gross.

Who said abuse is ugly?

It has a special kind of beauty

that you whimpering fools

will never be able to see.

So, go kill yourself

and set the world free

from your unwanted presence.

The world is not your kingdom

There's place for every person

You can bully me all you want

But I'm not going to run

You're blinded by Hate, my friend

But Hate is a beast with a limited lifespan

Sooner or later, it overplays its hand

That's when the game ends.

Hate is its own enemy

Don't be its willing slave

It's a free country

So, why choose to be in chains?

Despite all your toxicity,

I'm willing to shake hands.

It's never too late to make a change.

PS: With our social (media) spaces getting invaded by toxicity, I wanted to take a gritty look at the phenomenon of abuse through an intense poetic

dialogue. I imagined a confrontation between an abuser who is an unapologetic proponent of hate and a victim who can no longer be browbeaten into silence. The victim has made up her mind to face her tormentor and stand her ground, no matter what comes her way. This is how resistance truly begins. It is the point at which we propel a conversation on thorny subjects by refusing to be quiet. That's a crucial step for paving the pathway to a better and kinder world. I'm grateful to ThePrint for publishing this poem.

Part 2

The Theatre of Abuse

4

Well-intentioned Souls?

Playing their Part in the Drama of Abuse

It's such a blessing that this bleak world

is brimming with *well-intentioned* souls

for, if they could help it, would never want to hurt

even a polite pigeon

or a harmless human,

but so awful are the ways of the universe

that it contrives all manner of tribulations

by turning these gems among Homo sapiens

into puppets without a voice,

compelled to perform conversations

orchestrated by the puppeteer—

furiously pulling the strings—

robbing them of the power to resist

the command to live out a script

that they don't even get to fully read.

So, they keep their minds on the shelf

Enact their part fairly well

Leave the stage

and reclaim their normal selves.

Build walls in their troubled minds

that keep all scruples out of sight

while their unintentional cruelty wreaks havoc

in the life of some unfortunate being

whose every objection to their playacting
is promptly met with gaslighting,
leaving that suffering creature
to navigate the labyrinths of hell
while listening to the maddening chorus of
"All is well", "All is well", "All is well".
Voices so spectacularly misleading
that they make the sufferer's blood boil
with their unintentional deception
and genuine conviction
that they *do* mean well
even if their words are pure drivel,
summing up the ultimate tragedy
of this world full of people
overflowing with *good intentions*
that can light up the darkest of caverns
and yet end up creating
the landscape of hell.
But how do you even tell

these *well-intentioned* enablers

of subtle forms of torture

that their perpetual denial,

their comforting bubble

of self-justification,

bordering on self-deception,

may serve as a great defence mechanism,

but, with all their *good intentions*,

(forgive the repetition)

they will push a blameless person—

a casualty of their abject submission

and active participation

in the theatre of the absurd—

to the point of no return.

Every false word dropping from their lips

will exact a deadly toll

Dragging someone deeper and deeper

into a bottomless pit

till their last ray of hope is extinguished.

Oh, what a tragedy it is to be so *well-intentioned*

that someone you never wanted to hurt was "accidentally" killed.

5

Warped Webs

Toxic Games and Word-Traps

So, here we go again
I'm now done with this game
Not that I ever was a part
of this ridiculous charade.
I have sense enough not to be dragged
into this mind-numbing morass.

Nothing here is even remotely subtle
But those dragged into this theatre of abuse
Prefer to stay in their comfortable bubble
Quick to find refuge in denial
Before reality hits them in the face
A reality too painful for them to bear
Depressing though it is
It is what it is.

For those in the thick of this

The fine line that separates

Silly from sublime

Real from unreal

Genuine from gibberish

Ceases to exist.

This farce is so in-your-face

that it leaves me gasping for air.

I wish I could go back to living

my good old life—unruffled, unscathed.

But such is my predicament

that every earnest attempt

to winnow the chaff from the wheat

leaves me empty-handed.

All that seems to carry sense turns out in the end

to be nothing but a veiled assault

on my intelligence.

Still, I get trapped in this warped web of words

By the time I realise what's at work,

it is already too late.
The sinister word games
have injected their poison
into my veins.
Once it starts to take effect,
I feel the onslaught of pain
and the pounding in my head—
a constant irritant
in my blighted existence.

To those pulling the strings
and revelling in such madness,
I have a small request:
I am not a dumping ground
for the emotions you can't contain.
Why don't you have a word with God
and find a better way
to deal with whatever niggles at you
every minute of every day.
Maybe you're suffering too
But are afraid to confess

that there are feelings within you

that you simply cannot repress.

Perhaps it's too hard for you

to even admit to yourselves

that you must invent new ways

to escape the guilt

that, hopefully, accompanies

the injuries you inflict.

You're blinded by rage

that feeds on itself.

It keeps growing and growing

till you can no longer hold it in.

Little wonder, it is unleashed at whim.

Unlike you, I'm not afraid to appear weak

Nor am I excessively proud of the strength,

I've summoned to face adversity.

I don't mind sitting in the lap of misery

and bemoaning the precious time

lost in extracting sense

from all the word jugglery

devoid of substance.

Forgive my audacity
But it's time I tell you clearly
that you must let me be.
It is *my* life
And it is mine to live
You can play your tricks
till I cease to be
But even in death,
I will still be ME.
As long as I breathe,
I will cling tenaciously to that one real thing—
The sanctuary for my sanity
The place I find clarity
The thing called reality.

I hope you've heard of it.

6

A Tragic Apology

Victim, Enablers and the Irrationality of Abuse

What did I do to deserve this?
These piercing barbs, mocking memes,
vicious gossip, whisper campaigns—
tearing apart my psyche,
every single day.

Why do you do what you do?

We know we've not been good to you

And we keenly feel your pain too

This is something we never wanted to do

But the concoction of lies, half-truths and rumours

perplexed us beyond words.

Spurred on by some crazy notion,

we lost our inner compass.

Then why don't you stop, once and for all?
Every awakening is accompanied by a fall
Why do you keep lingering on the edge of hell?
You're killing me and disfiguring your soul.

We don't mean to hurt you.

You are loved. You are like us.

But, you see, there are commands

that come from above.

What do you mean by "above"?
Does God tell you to follow instructions at
loggerheads with his own lessons?
Is he breathing down your spine,
which is already broken?

No, it's not God. It's the one in charge.

In charge of what, in the name of the Lord?

In charge of our safety.

Your safety? Who's harming you?

The Other.

Did you say "brother"?
Or "neighbour"?
Or the "weather"?
Will you pardon my ears
and repeat the answer.

The Other.

What have I got to do with this "Other"—
the target of your vacuous ire—
if I may venture to enquire?

YOU are the Other.

But, you admitted, I'm just like you.

In a way, that is true.

We kind of feel that too.

Be we must conform

if we have to belong.

Do I not belong?

Maybe you do.

But we've been told to close ranks

to protect ourselves from you.

Protect? Where is the threat?

There is. Apparently, there is.

That's the general consensus.

We need to be afraid.

We must stay on our guard.

That's we've heard.

That's what is said.

There's something like that.

That's what we know ...

We don't really know ...

But there is something, it seems ...

So, you're frightened by some morbid fantasy
Gripped by paranoia
Ready to relinquish your humanity
for ... what did you say? Oh, yeah right, "safety",
whatever that means in your vocabulary.
So, you are decent people driven crazy by the
phantom of fear
You're all kind, very kind
It's just that you're losing your mind
So, I must be patient and let you walk all over
me.

These are dark times

Everyone's changing

We're being carried along

where the wind is blowing.

But it's getting too much for us too.

We'll have to make amends

for what we made you go through.

We promise to bring you a band-aid

that can be applied to all wounds.

Even those festering in one's heart?
And what about the scars
that will bear witness to the barbarity
of this man-made calamity?
But let's leave that aside
Because no answer will suffice
I'll have to live with my wounds
There's no magic balm
for the injuries you've caused,
injuries of which I've now lost count.

Would an apology make you feel good?

Oh, yes, that really helps.

So, when are you going to enable abuse next?

Be kind enough to keep me informed.

It takes me some time to put my armour on.

This will end. We won't be a party to this nonsense.

Why do I feel I've heard this before?

A thousand times at least, if not more.

Never again. Never again.

Yes, you won't do this again.

Until of course the orders are sent.

Then you'll be a good soldier

and attack a defenceless innocent.

Maybe even your own girlfriend.

You've lost your agency with your irresolution

Muddled your heads with made-up confusion

I know you all have "good intentions"

But, somehow, they don't get reflected in your actions.

Yet, you seem to be cast in a decent mould

But it might just break when the next rock is hurled.

In case I don't get up after the fall,

please show your humanity by attending my funeral.

PS: This is an intense poetic dialogue between an individual and his compatriots, who have labelled him as the Other. The individual's only fault is that he doesn't belong to the majority community. This becomes reason enough to view him with suspicion and attack him without provocation. Though his fellow humans have been swayed by misleading rhetoric, the voice of their conscience refuses to be suppressed. They are, however, too confused to apologise with unwavering conviction—the tragedy of indoctrination. I wrote this poem as a keen observer of society, with a PhD that examines the possibility of peace and mutual care in an increasingly volatile and violent world.

I'm grateful to ThePrint for publishing this poem.

Part 3

Difficult Dynamics

7

The Big, Blinding Ego

A Stifling Relationship Slowly Unspools

You don't even know the injuries you've inflicted

by your sheer arrogance and an ego so inflated

that the slightest attempt to dispute your self-certified truths

are viewed as nothing less than a monumental insult.

Your commanding style skilfully conceals

the timid figure you are underneath.

Ready to mouth inanities

to safeguard your own peace.

Despite our differences, I have wanted to love you

and hoped to be loved in return.

But you don't have the clear-sighted courage

to support me in the long run.

I'm tired of your angst and the accompanying verbiage

I'm sorry but you often fail to make sense

And I am better off keeping my distance

I've tried to get across my point

But it has all been in vain

You're not the one who would deign to listen

or ever be willing to change.

Despite the occasional praise,

you're wedded to your ways.

So, there is really no space

for me to have my say.

You've not abused me

Nor even wanted to hurt me

You've been polite to a fault

And yet you have often

disappointed me beyond words.

So terribly sad is this situation

that it admits no open-hearted communication.

Like a speck of dust, your ego

obstructs your vision.

It is tragic but true

And there's nothing I can do.

You've hurt me, more often than is fair

I've had no option but to swallow the words

you wouldn't even bother to hear.

In my world, you were a fixture

Now you seem like a familiar stranger

who used to be quite close.

Even that closeness has been lost

And all that is left is pain

A pain too deep for me to measure

A pain that will remain.

Our relationship has lost its imperfect rhythm
And it will never be the same again.

The place I kept in my heart for you
will eventually be taken by someone
who doesn't hurt me constantly
the way you have often done.
I hope to always see you happy
But I can't handle the toxicity
that assails me the moment
you're in my vicinity.
I doubt you have the humility
to look within and reflect.

That would be too much to expect.

You are guilty of causing so much hurt

But your ego, your gigantic ego,
would never let you admit
that there are things you should repent.
With a dismissive shrug,
you'll trivialize my wounds
and offer gratuitous lessons.
You think you've grown too wise
to be subjected to criticism.
So, spare me your hypocrisy
by talking about democracy.
I'm tired of the way you impose
your contentious views on me.
I can't take it anymore
I just can't do it
So, I'll keep to myself.

Don't remember to call me
Let us part ways and forget

the bittersweet moments

that have torn our bond to shreds.

You live the way you deem fit

But don't shoehorn me into your mould

I have to find my own way

And life has to go on …

God knows that I tried

But we weren't meant to get along.

8

No Room for Differences

Spells Doom for Relationships

Your views contrast with mine

And that's perfectly fine

No two creatures on this Earth

are so wondrously alike

that everything before their eyes

takes on the same guise

and, as a marvellous coincidence,

is seen in the same light.

So, if you're attached to your point of view

I really don't mind

I'm unique and so are you

So, where's the need to fight?

Why argue with the sole aim

to gain your point?

Why do you always hesitate

to open up space for a passionate debate?

If I hold on to my own take,

why should that be a grave mistake?

I've been through hell so many times

You don't even know the hills I've climbed

Every time I've ventured to speak my mind

Your eyes glaze over

Evincing your obvious disinterest

in things that truly matter.

So, I think I've had enough

of your pretence of concern.

Whenever I'm with you,

I lose my inner peace.

Never have our conversations

flowed with ease.

You are not the wisest

in this wide, wild world

that leaves one dazed

with its twists and turns.

And I am not a prophet

with an unerring instinct

that can foresee the best course

for a life that is still unfolding—

a life with a life of its own.

We're mere mortals stumbling through life

We are bound to make mistakes

And yet, you always have to be right

Hell-bent on having the final say.

Despite your proclamations of humility,

you betray your deep-seated belief

in your sense of superiority.

Your heart is not big enough to forgive

anything that even appears as a slight.

You simply refuse to let go and forget

Nursing resentments that don't make sense

At moments like this, I must confess

you mildly resemble an autocrat

that gets affronted by someone's assertions

that challenge their rigid convictions.

So, it's no surprise that the same old nonsense
rears its head every now and then.
And once again with stinging politeness
you repeat what you have said
so often that it is bound to offend
anyone with a modicum of self-respect.

And yet you can't get out of your head
things that have been discussed to death.
I know better now than to reason with you
It's simply a waste of breath

You are what you are

And there's nothing more to be said.

Part 4

Wounds Deep Within

9

A Strange Predicament

A Victim Wonders Why the Suffering Never Ends

There's no way this can continue!

Why, of all the people, did they choose YOU
to let loose their volley of abuse?

I no longer think why they do what they do

Battered and bruised, I still get a kick or two

It's happened so often that I've forgotten to pause

and wonder at the imaginary cause

for the vicious onslaught

that needs no provocation

and comes without invitation.

But why? For heaven's sake, why?

Forget about justification

Don't tax your imagination

It makes no sense!

That's the whole point, my friend

It's the epitome of nonsense

The crystallized essence of malevolence

The purest form of pettiness

The pinnacle of absurdity

The definition of cruelty.

Well, I can't watch this without raising my voice.

I'll advise you to be careful

Lest you be dragged through hell

For the crime of speaking sense

I don't want you to be trapped in this warped web

It's probably worse than being dead

Although I'm used to all this by now

A voice inside me still screams out—

"Help! Help!"

Though I know better than to waste words

on the gas-lighters of this deceptive world,

it doesn't lesson my agony.

I hope you're luckier than me

and are spared the exquisite torment

of watching this tragicomedy.

Though my mind resists thinking

about these myriad shades of inhumanity,

laced with inanity, bordering on insanity,

I have reluctantly formed my own theory

about these proclivities

among people who seem like you and me.

If you're patient enough, I'll venture to share

the insights gained from the depths of despair.

The questions woven into my formulation

spring from my trials and tribulations.

Don't mistake these howls of anguish for mere rhetoric.

You may need to ask some questions too

if you have the grave misfortune

of routinely getting a kick or two

by the minions of those lords

who trample people underfoot

as a macabre sport.

It's a way those kings massage their egos,

more fragile than a baby's fingers,

held intact by ruling over

and keeping under a tight leash

whoever they meet and greet.

No one escapes their iron grip

They'll not let their control slip

Man, they're sharp and insanely quick

They have a storehouse of dirty tricks

Their whims reign supreme—

To hell with morality!

To hell with the means!

Never let yourself be dragged into their dungeon.

So, please read with your eyes wide open—

Once kicking the weak and the meek
or the ones keen to avoid conflict
becomes too frequent to make you stop and think,
the pangs of conscience that once gave you pause
have long been suppressed and no longer prick.
You've forgotten where your moral compass was
You haven't consulted it for far too long
The qualms and scruples are a thing of the past
And yet, you have some light within
You haven't completely given in
The empathy your leader inherently lacks
tis woven into the fabric of your being.
Even when cruelty reigns supreme,
humanity is not so easily shed.
It is bound to rear its head.
And so, you're ambushed by guilt
despite all the walls you've built
to escape the intense discomfort

that comes with causing hurt.

Enabling abuse may seem like a compulsion

when you're confronted with the guillotine.

It may not seem like a choice

And the aftereffects might make you want to cry.

This world is enslaved by tyrants

who invent news ways to torment

people who can't stand up to them.

They pit human against human,

turning them into victims, tools and weapons.

But sooner or later, reality sinks in.

Maybe the enablers have their share of suffering

And yet, they must face the moment of reckoning—

that moment when the world stops spinning

and sanity reasserts itself.

It's sad how they can't resist someone

bending them to their ill-will.

Maybe they try to stand their ground

Maybe they side with the devil

Maybe they feel helpless,

which may be true or a lame excuse.

Either way, it doesn't cut much ice

How hard is it to just be nice?

To become the purveyors of borrowed malice

is simply tragic.

And yet, there's no dearth of enablers

doing the bidding of their diabolical masters,

following orders like loyal soldiers,

believing in the legitimacy of their cause

even when they feel it's mere eyewash.

They've given over their power

and now it seems …

They're stuck in a quagmire.

They know they can do better

but still they cut a sorry figure

over and over.

Even the sufferer feels mortified

by their abject servility.

As if they were at the mercy

of the one holding the reins

and passing orders that must be obeyed.

Maybe they, too, feel pain

and don't deserve all the blame.

Their intentions may not be bad, but, tell me,

how does that help?

How do they go on living when they know
someone is bleeding?

How do they bring themselves to knock them down
again and again?

Tell me, friend, does it make any sense

to victimise the innocent?

It defies logic

And, yes, it is tragic.

There are questions galore

And, I'm not afraid to stick out my neck

And say the things that need to be said

Holding fast to reason

and the moral emotions

that make us human.

I would entreat the enablers of all things horrible

to break out of their denial

and do the world the kindness of speaking with candour

about a matter

staring in the eye

and demanding an immediate answer.

Why, in God's name, do you allow yourself to be used,

knowing full well that you'll leave someone with wounds

that may heal with time

or fester all their life?

Don't answer me

Answer Him: The One above

In case you got me wrong,

I'm talking about God

Not the High and Almighty you've learnt to obey

But The One who represents all that is good and fair

Answer him

Answer him someday.

10

The Complex Web of Tyranny

If a Victim Could Hold a Mirror to Their Tormentor

I don't speak because I expect you to change

Nor do I even wish to be heard

That was all in the distant past

When my hopes had not been crushed

Now I live because I must

And still hope for a better world

Because hope is all there is

Even when you're bruised and burned.

After all is said and done

and mournful silence reigns,

one final wish will still remain—

that you wouldn't even attempt to explain

what permits no explanation.

Let remorse wash over you

and make you feel the pain

you've caused innocent people

time and time again.

You've insulted reason, killed compassion

Maybe it calls for some reflection

Maybe.

Maybe you don't have the power to decide

And your hands are, unfortunately, tied

Forcing you to become a vehicle

for someone else's spite.

I hope there is a gulf between your actions

and what you feel inside.

But, tell me friend, how does that help

if it destroys countless lives?

So, let us agree that you're sorry

but that sorry will not suffice.

The wounds you've inflicted heartlessly

won't heal in the blink of an eye.

You know this as well as I do,

and sometimes I actually feel bad for you.

Maybe you're not allowed the option

to disobey the order to be cruel.

Even if that can pass off as an excuse

And is indisputably true

I hope you'll be sensible enough

to know it wouldn't do.

Because some things are inexcusable

even if there is a "reason".

Though I no longer dare to expect

anything from anyone,

I still have one small request

if only you would care to listen.

You can't rewrite the past

What's done is done!

Just remember to hold yourself to account

for every single injury inflicted without a cause

Ask yourself tough questions

Don't try to cheat your conscience

Think of what you've become

by your blind obedience.

The howls of anguish you blithely ignored

Will echo through the years

What's done can *never* be undone

Your actions will haunt you, me and everyone

for a very long time to come.

So, stop this madness in God's name

And NEVER let it happen again.

NEVER AGAIN.

PS: This is a poem on the insufferable cruelty in Gaza that is unfolding before our very eyes. No torture, large-scale violence, genocidal acts, and the like are possible without the complicity of an army of players who owe allegiance to a tyrannical regime and execute its evil designs. This comes into conflict with the fact that empathy is a capacity that human beings have possessed for ages, as strongly backed by research. So, how do the foot soldiers of an autocrat bring themselves to follow cruel instructions? This is a poem calling into question the compliance and complicity of people, many of whom may be like you and me, that enables crimes against humanity.

I'm grateful to ThePrint for publishing this poem.

Epilogue

The Final Word

You think I'm fine

Because my wounds cannot be seen

But if you could see my psyche

riddled with injuries

You might think differently.

In one sense, I'm fine

I'm breathing

My heart is beating

My appetite is abysmal

But I'm still eating

I can still sleep well

Thanks to the pills

My brain hasn't exploded

Which is a miracle

Despite the unbearable pain,

I haven't burst a blood vessel

Although I have headaches,

That are terrible.

I am performing the act of living

And I am technically alive

Even if something inside me has died.

I drag myself out of the bed

Every single day

I go through the motions

Act like a functional human

I'm almost intact

And yet, I'm broken

But that's something better left unsaid

We have to live with our fate—

Fair or unfair.

What rankles is the ease with which we forget

It does not have to be this way.

Acknowledgements

I am greatly indebted to *ThePrint* for unhesitatingly providing a platform for some of the hard-hitting poems in this collection. Their willingness to publish my work gave me the confidence to go ahead and publish a collection on a difficult issue. I'm deeply obliged to my manager, Mr Mukesh, for his constant support.

On the personal front, I am immensely grateful to my elder brother, who has become the wind beneath my wings. My dearest Vaibhav, you have been my rock and emotional anchor after Papa passed away. Your love has been as unconditional as that of our parents, and your unwavering support has meant the world to me.

A big hug to Parakram for worrying and caring for me even when I wasn't the easiest person to get along with.

Dr Anil Jain, you continue to be our go-to person in sickness and health. Whenever there is a medical crisis, your advice is invaluable. Dr

Jitendra, you are as supportive as always, and I hope our long association continues.

Finally, a big thank you to Mama and Papa for being the most loving parents in the world. You both are always in my heart. Because of you, I know the purest form of love. Papa, I hope you are watching me from above with a sense of pride. I am sure your passion for electrons and electricity has outlived your earthly existence. But more than that, I feel your immeasurable love for me has remained intact. I feel that love in my very bones, making it possible for me to carry on.

Mama, I feel stronger because you are still around. You're an invisible force that keeps me going when the chips are down. Nothing compares to mother-love. Nothing compares to *your* love. I love you as much—and much more than words can convey.